1 *There are many ways of completing this question. Either of the specimen completions below would receive full marks.*   (15)

EITHER

(a) *Chords are shown here with roman numerals AND notes on the stave. EITHER of these methods of notation would receive full marks. Other recognized methods of notation will also be considered and marks awarded accordingly.*

OR

(b)

2 *There are many ways of completing this question. The specimen completion below would receive full marks.* (15)

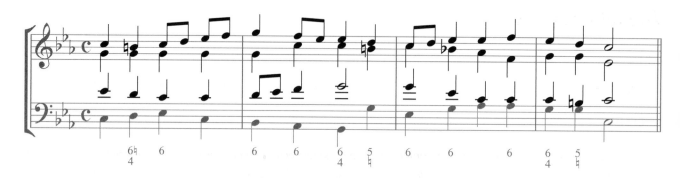

3 *There are many ways of completing this question. Either of the specimen completions below would receive full marks.* (20) *The given openings are printed in grey in order to distinguish them from the completion, but candidates must include the opening in their answer.*

EITHER

(a) *Source: Schumann, Piano Quartet in E flat major, Op. 47*

cello

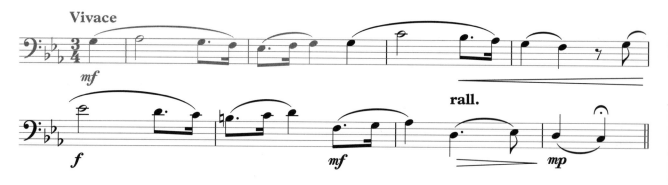

OR

(b) oboe

4 (a) moderately slow / rather slow   (4)

   one string / left pedal / press the left pedal   (2)

(b) Bar 14 ii°⁷b / II⁷b diminished / iv⁶a / IV⁶a minor   (6)

   Bar 15 V⁷a / V⁷a major

(c) Similarity melody / articulation of melody / both begin $\boldsymbol{p}$ (1)

   One mark will be awarded (up to a maximum of two marks) for each correct reference to the following: (2)
   Differences melody an octave lower / melody in left-hand part / grace note in bar 3 /
   hairpin dynamics / harmony / poco espr. in bar 25 / thinner texture in bars 25–28 /
   quaver rests

(d) *All possible answers are shown on the extract reproduced below. For full marks, candidates need to identify only one example of each answer.*

   B Bars 19–20   (2)

   C Bar 14   (2)

   D Bar 19 / 23   (2)

   E Bar(s) 17 / 17–18 / 18   (2)

(e) major 6th   (2)

5 *Source: Howard Ferguson, Octet, Op. 4*

    (a) down-bow / play from the heel of the bow   (2)

        getting quicker / gradually getting quicker / getting faster / gradually getting faster   (2)

        plucked   (2)

    (b) (i)   Clarinet   (4)

       (ii)   Horn   (3)

    (c) *All possible answers are shown on the extract reproduced below. For full marks, candidates need to identify only one example of each answer.*

        B Bar 8   (2)

        C Bar 6 / 7   (2)

        D Bar 7   (2)

    (d) **1** diminished 4th   (2)

       2 minor 2nd   (2)

    (e) true   (2)

Music Theory Practice Papers 2017

Model Answers

ABRSM Grade 6

Welcome to ABRSM's *Music Theory Practice Papers 2017 Model Answers*, Grade 6. These answers are a useful resource for students and teachers preparing for ABRSM theory exams and should be used alongside the relevant published theory practice papers.

All the answers in this booklet would receive full marks but not all possible answers have been included for practicable reasons. In these cases other reasonable alternatives may also be awarded full marks. For composition-style questions only one example of the many possible answers is given.

For more information on how theory papers are marked and some general advice on taking theory exams, please refer to **www.abrsm.org/theory**.

Using these answers

- Answers are given in the same order and, where possible, in the same layout as in the exam papers, making it easy to match answer to question.

- Where it is necessary to show the answer on a stave, the original stave is printed in grey with the answer shown in black, for example:

- Alternative answers are shown in one of three ways:

    1. separated by an oblique stroke (/), for example: V^7c / V^7c major

    2. by using *or*, for example:

    3. by using boxes where the definition of a phrase consists of two or more terms. Correct answers may be constructed by selecting any one option from each box, as in this example:

    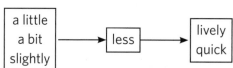

- American note names, for example half note and quarter note, are accepted but have not been included in the answers as they are not used in the exam papers.

- Where the source of an excerpt is not identified in full in the question paper, it is given at the start of the answer to enable candidates to consult the original. The specimen answers do not necessarily follow the composer's original.

- Extended roman and basic roman numerals are used in answers that require chord identification.

- The old-style crotchet rest ≹ is accepted as a valid alternative to the modern symbol ≩ .

- Sometimes the clef, key and time signature of the relevant bar(s) are included for added clarity, for example:

© 2018 by The Associated Board of the Royal Schools of Music
Published by ABRSM (Publishing) Ltd, a wholly owned subsidiary of ABRSM
Cover by Kate Benjamin & Andy Potts
Printed in England by Halstan & Co. Ltd, Amersham, Bucks, on materials from sustainable sources

Theory Paper   Grade 6   2017   B
Model Answers

1 *There are many ways of completing this question. Either of the specimen completions below would receive full marks.*   (15)

EITHER

(a) *Chords are shown here with roman numerals AND notes on the stave. EITHER of these methods of notation would receive full marks. Other recognized methods of notation will also be considered and marks awarded accordingly.*

*	*	*_____*	*	*_____*	*	*	*	*	*	*	*	*	*	*
Ia	Vb	Ia	iib	via	iiia	IVa	Ia	via	Va	Ib	iib	Ic	Va	Ia

OR

(b)

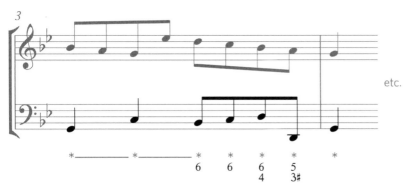

etc.

2 *There are many ways of completing this question. The specimen completion below would receive full marks.* (15)

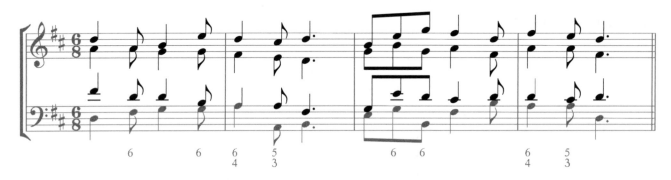

3 *There are many ways of completing this question. Either of the specimen completions below would receive full marks.* (20) *The given openings are printed in grey in order to distinguish them from the completion, but candidates must include the opening in their answer.*

EITHER

(a) *Source: Haydn, String Quartet in D major, Op. 20 No. 4*

clarinet

OR

(b) trumpet

4 (a) slow / stately (2)

(b) (i) 13 (2)

    (ii) viola; second violin (2)

(c) Bar 3 ii^{7}b / II^{7}b minor / IV^{6}a / IV^{6}a major (3)

    Bar 15 V^{7}a / V^{7}a major (3)

(d) *All possible answers are shown on the extract reproduced below. For full marks, candidates need to identify only one*
   example of each answer.

   B Bar 9   (2)

   C Bar 7 / 8   (2)

   D Bar 4   (2)

(e)    (3)

(f) (i)   false   (2)

   (ii)   false   (2)

5 (a) majestic / stately (2)

playful / joking (2)

on the G string (2)

(b) (i) Clarinets (2)

(ii) Horns $\frac{1}{2}$ (4)

(c) (i) C♭; first flute; 5 (3)

(ii) second violins (2)

(iii) trombone / tuba (2)

(iv) 6 (2)

(v) 10 (2)

(d) true (2)

Theory Paper   Grade 6   2017   C
Model Answers

1 *There are many ways of completing this question. Either of the specimen completions below would receive full marks.* (15)

EITHER

(a) *Chords are shown here with roman numerals AND notes on the stave. EITHER of these methods of notation would receive full marks. Other recognized methods of notation will also be considered and marks awarded accordingly.*

OR

(b)

2 *There are many ways of completing this question. The specimen completion below would receive full marks.* (15)

3 *There are many ways of completing this question. Either of the specimen completions below would receive full marks.* (20)
The given openings are printed in grey in order to distinguish them from the completion, but candidates must include the opening in their answer.

EITHER

(a) *Source (adapted): Haydn, String Quartet in B minor, Op. 33 No. 1*

violin

OR

(b) trombone

4 *Source: Clementi, Piano Sonata Op. 8 No. 3*

(a) Bar 3   iib / IIb minor (3)

   Bar 6   V⁷c / V⁷c major (3)

(b) *All possible answers are shown on the extract reproduced opposite. For full marks, candidates need to identify only one example of each answer.*

   B Bars 11–12 (2)

   C Bar 21 (2)

   D Bar(s) 12–13 / 13 / 14 (2)

   E Bar 10 (2)

   F Bar 20 (2)

   G Bar 16 / 20 (2)

(c) (i)   F; 16   (2)

   (ii)   C minor   (2)

   (iii) B♭ minor   (2)

(d)   1750–1850   (1)

5 *Source: Mahler, Symphony No. 1 in D major (original version)*

   (a) on the G string   (2)

        slide / slide from one note to the next   (2)

        tender / delicate / soft   (2)

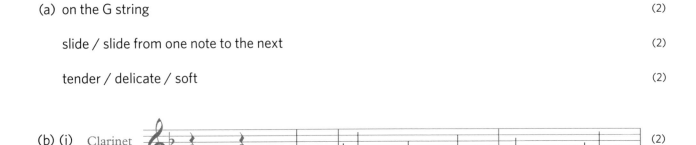

   (b) (i) Clarinet   (2)

   (ii) Horns ½   (2)

(c) *All possible answers are shown on the extract reproduced below. For full marks, candidates need to identify only one example of each answer.*

B Bars 8–9 / 9–10 (2)

C Bar 10 (2)

D Bars 6–9 (2)

(d) (i) 7; 8 (2)

(ii) minor 6th (2)

(e) (i) true (2)

(ii) true (2)

(f) <u>Mahler</u> (1)

Theory Paper   Grade 6   2017   S
Model Answers

1 *There are many ways of completing this question. Either of the specimen completions below would receive full marks.*   (15)

EITHER

(a) *Chords are shown here with roman numerals AND notes on the stave. EITHER of these methods of notation would receive full marks. Other recognized methods of notation will also be considered and marks awarded accordingly.*

OR

(b)

2 *There are many ways of completing this question. The specimen completion below would receive full marks.* (15)

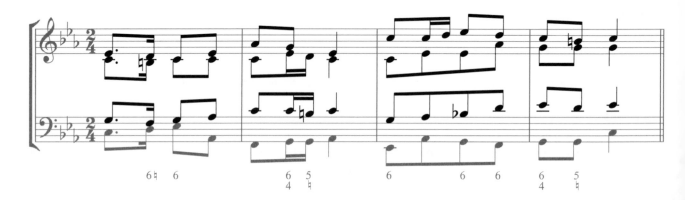

3 *There are many ways of completing this question. Either of the specimen completions below would receive full marks.* (20)
The given openings are printed in grey in order to distinguish them from the completion, but candidates must include the opening in their answer.

EITHER

(a) *Source (adapted): Schubert, Symphony No. 2 in B flat major, D.125*

trumpet

OR

(b) flute

4 (a) peaceful / tranquil / calm / serene (2)

(b) **X** accented passing note (2)

Y lower auxiliary note / chromatic lower auxiliary note (2)

Z acciaccatura / grace note / crushed note (2)

(c) Bar 17 V^7b / V^7b major (3)

Bar 19 ii^7a / II^7a minor / IV^6d / IV^6d major (3)

(d) Similarities dynamics / melodic shape (2)

One mark will be awarded (up to a maximum of three marks) for each correct reference to the following: (3)

Differences accent in bar 14 / melody at lower pitch in bars 13–14 / key / left-hand part all in octaves in bars 13–14 / rhythm in bar 13

(e) *All possible answers are shown on the extract reproduced below.*

B Bar 18 (2)

C Bars 16–17 (2)

D Bar 12 (2)

5 (a) plucked (2)

(b) (i) Clarinet 1  (3)

(ii) Horn  (2)

(c) *All possible answers are shown on the extract reproduced on the opposite page. For full marks, candidates need to identify only one example of each answer.*

    B Bar(s) 5 / 6–7 (2)

    C Bars 8–9 (2)

    D Bar 11 (2)

(d) cellos; second violins; horn; second clarinet (4)

(e) bassoon (2)

(f) (i) false (2)

    (ii) false (2)

    (iii) true (2)

19

Music Theory Practice Papers 2017 Model Answers

Model answers for four practice papers from ABRSM's 2017 Music Theory exams for Grade 6

Key features:

- a list of correct answers where appropriate
- a selection of likely options where the answer can be expressed in a variety of ways
- a single exemplar where a composition-style answer is required

Support material for ABRSM Music Theory exams

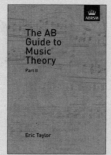

Supporting the teaching and learning of music in partnership with the Royal Schools of Music

Royal Academy of Music | Royal College of Music
Royal Northern College of Music | Royal Conservatoire of Scotland

ISBN 978-1-78601-014-8

9 781786 010148

www.abrsm.org   f facebook.com/abrsm
🐦 @abrsm   ▶ ABRSM YouTube